HAL LEONARD SONGWRITING METHOD

BY TOM HAMBRIDGE

PLAYBACK➕
Speed • Pitch • Balance • Loop

To access audio, visit:
www.halleonard.com/mylibrary

Enter Code
7173-7016-8191-5079

Front cover photo: Rachel Hambridge

ISBN 978-1-70510-414-9

HAL•LEONARD®

Visit Hal Leonard Online at
www.halleonard.com

World headquarters, contact:
Hal Leonard
7777 West Bluemound Road
Milwaukee, WI 53213
Email: info@halleonard.com

In Europe, contact:
Hal Leonard Europe Limited
1 Red Place
London, W1K 6PL
Email: info@halleonardeurope.com

In Australia, contact:
Hal Leonard Australia Pty. Ltd.
4 Lentara Court
Cheltenham, Victoria, 3192 Australia
Email: info@halleonard.com.au

FOREWORD

If you're holding this book, you've been wondering how to write a song, or how to take your songwriting to the next level. This book lays out all the tips, tricks, and fundamentals for lyric writing and music arranging for your song. These are the very same tried and true practices used by songwriters for decades in every popular musical genre. But they are not all the rules, because in songwriting, there are no rules. You get to decide which rules to follow, and which ones to break. What I love about songwriting are the discoveries you make once you get started.

Don't ever let yourself be overwhelmed by the idea of writing a song, because every songwriter starts with the same blank page and the same quiet instruments. What makes a song special is when you strike the instrument in your own unique style, sharing what's on your mind and what's in your heart. There are many clever ways to craft a song, as this book will reveal, but there remains an infinite amount of cathartic, important ways to reveal some deep truths about love, life, and the world that only you will discover in your musical journey. The more you practice, the quicker the ideas will seem to flow through you. I've written great songs in minutes, but I've also labored over ideas for more than a decade before finally breathing enough life to realize what was best for the song.

If I can offer any advice, it's this: keep writing. Maybe it's a song a week, or for the adventurous, it's a song a day (after all, nothing inspires like a deadline). The more you write, you'll find that one song leads you to the next one, then on to the best one yet. Or you may take an idea from one of your older songs to make something new. Again, there are no rules. And there's no wasted effort. Just keep writing! And have fun. After all, we don't work music—we play music.

Good luck,

Jason Mraz

INTRODUCTION

Hal Leonard Songwriting Method is designed to teach everyone at any level or any age how to find an idea, develop that idea, and create a song out of it. You do not have to be a great musician or singer. It doesn't matter whether you can play an instrument or not. Anyone who has ever dreamed, wanted, or thought about writing a song can do it. This book will teach you how.

ABOUT THE AUTHOR

Tom Hambridge is a Grammy®-winning singer, songwriter, producer, and drummer.

Tom's production work includes duets or solo projects with: B.B. King, Eric Clapton, Buddy Guy, Gregg Allman, Keith Richards, Keb Mo, Susan Tedeschi, Carlos Santana, Steven Tyler & Joe Perry of Aerosmith, Van Morrison, Mick Jagger, Keith Urban, James Bay, Kid Rock, Foghat, Billy Gibbons, Warren Haynes, Derek Trucks, James Cotton, George Thorogood, Gary Clark Jr., Jeff Beck, Joss Stone, Allen Toussaint, Delbert McClinton, Johnny Winter, Marcia Ball, Kingfish, Quinn Sullivan, Kenny Neal, and many others.

Tom has had over 600 of his songs recorded by such diverse artists as B.B. King, ZZ Top, Lynyrd Skynyrd, Meatloaf, Billy Ray Cyrus, Foghat, Rascal Flatts, Chris Young, Gretchen Wilson, Keb Mo, George Thorogood, Rodney Atkins, Joe Nichols, Montgomery Gentry, Van Zant, Ronnie Dunn, The Outlaws, Johnny Winter, John Mayall, Eric Burden, Joe Bonamassa, Jamey Johnson, and many others. His songs have been included in many major motion pictures, TV movies and shows, from *American Idol* and *Criminal Minds* to the Super Bowl.

Tom has produced nine Grammy®-nominated albums and has won four Grammy® Awards, countless Handy and Blues Music Awards, nine Boston Music Awards, and ASCAP Country Music Awards. He is a recipient of the prestigious KBA Award in Memphis (Keeping the Blues Alive) and has been inducted into the Buffalo Music Hall of Fame.

As an artist, Tom has released eight solo albums, including *The Nola Sessions*, which won "Blues Album of the Year" Independent Music Awards.

As a drummer, Tom has played on albums and/or toured with Chuck Berry, Bo Diddley, Roy Buchanan, Boston, B.B. King, Mick Jagger, Eric Clapton, Susan Tedeschi, Buddy Guy, Hank Williams Jr., Delbert McClinton, George Thorogood and The Destroyers, Jeff Beck, James Cotton and many others.

CHAPTER 1: WORDS

THE CHICKEN OR THE EGG

What comes first: the music or the words?

There are no hard and fast rules. You can write the words first and then find or fit a chord progression to match the words. You can also play a series of chords (example below) and try to hum or sing syllables or nonsensical words and phrases until you come across words that sound good over the chords. This may trigger a story line or an idea that you can start to develop. When Paul McCartney was writing "Yesterday," he played the chords over and over and sang "Scrambled Eggs." It was a placeholder until he finally came up with "Yesterday."

Chord progressions to sing to
In the key of G major:
G, D, Em, C

In the key of C major:
C, F, G

In the key of C major:
C, G, Am, F

CO-WRITING

When two or more songwriters collaborate to create a song, it is called **co-writing**. Songwriters get together and try to come up with an idea to work on. Co-writing can be beneficial, because your co-writer may hear the melody a bit differently or have a different perspective to writing the lyric. As the saying goes, "Two heads are better than one." Many times, both writers contribute musical ideas as well as words, but sometimes one will write words only and the other will write the music only.

This co-writing can also be done separately. Bernie Taupin wrote lyrics and sent them to Elton John to write the music. "Tiny Dancer," "Your Song," "Don't Let the Sun Go Down on Me," "Rocket Man," and many others were written like this. Burt Bacharach and Hal David also used this approach: Hal wrote the words and Burt wrote the music. Some of the hits they wrote this way include: "Raindrops Keep Fallin' on My Head," "(They Long to Be) Close to You," and "One Less Bell to Answer."

Famous co-writers and some examples of songs they have co-written:
John Lennon and Paul McCartney
"Help!"
"Can't Buy Me Love"
"Let It Be"
"All You Need Is Love"

Gerry Goffin and Carole King
"Will You Love Me Tomorrow (Will You Still Love Me Tomorrow)"
"The Loco-Motion"
"Up on the Roof"

Mick Jagger and Keith Richards
"Honky Tonk Woman"
"Satisfaction"
"Paint It Black"
"Wild Horses"

Walter Becker and Donald Fagen
"Rikki Don't Lose That Number"
"Do It Again"
"Reelin' in the Years"
"Peg"

Isaac Hayes and David Porter
"Hold On, I'm Comin'"
"Soul Man"
"I Thank You"
"When Something Is Wrong with My Baby"

HOW TO START

Song ideas are all around us. Keep your ears and eyes open.

Phrases people say, idioms, and old sayings can make great song titles.

Examples: Every dog has its day, it had to be you, thinking out loud, rock the boat, best of both worlds, time after time, opposites attract.

Example lyric from "Opposites Attract," a duet by Susan Tedeschi and Tom Hambridge

I like to pitch
She lets me catch her
He wants the salt
She wants the pepper
He barks like a dog
She purrs like a pussy cat
Yeah, opposites attract

INSPIRATION

Inspiration doesn't always happen at the most convenient time. If you get an idea, it's good to write it down so you don't forget it. Or sing the words into your phone. Songs come from a million different places. Ideas are all around us. An idea can come from something someone says, a line in a TV show or movie you are watching. Suddenly, you have an idea for a song. You can also write about social injustice, an historical moment or empowerment.

Examples of songs based on historical events
"Ohio" (Crosby, Stills, Nash & Young)
"Ludlow Massacre" (Woody Guthrie)
"We Didn't Start the Fire" (Billy Joel)
"Let Him Dangle" (Elvis Costello)

Examples of songs about women's empowerment
"I'm Every Woman" (Chaka Khan)
"Flawless" (Beyonce)
"Respect" (Aretha Franklin)
"I Will Survive" (Gloria Gaynor)
"Man! I Feel Like a Woman!" (Shania Twain)
"Your Dog" (Soccer Mommy)

Examples of songs about social injustice
"Blowin' in the Wind" (Bob Dylan)
(This song has been referred to as an anti-war song as well as a Civil Rights anthem.)
"We Shall Overcome" (Pete Seeger)
"Strange Fruit" (Abel Meeropol)
(A Civil Rights song that describes black victims of lynchings as "strange fruit" that is hanging from the trees.)
"A Change Is Gonna Come" (Sam Cooke)

SONG LYRIC CONTENT

Words in songs are called **lyrics**.

You can write about a specific incident or story you have experienced in your own life or an incident that happened to someone else, a story you read about or heard about. You can even invent your own story. Make up your own characters.

Examples of songs inspired by true events or specific people:

"The Wreck of the Edmund Fitzgerald" (Gordon Lightfoot)
This song is about the sinking of the bulk carrier SS Edmund Fitzgerald on Lake Superior on November 10, 1975.

"Candle in the Wind" (Elton John)
This song was written to honor Marilyn Monroe. In 1997, Elton John adapted the song to honor Princess Diana, and sang it at her funeral.

"Hurricane" (Bob Dylan)
This song is about boxer Rubin "Hurricane" Carter who was falsely accused and convicted of murder. After spending ten years in prison, his conviction was overturned and he was released.

"American Pie" (Don McLean)
This song, with the phrase "the day the music died," is about the plane crash that killed Buddy Holly, Richie Valens, and The Big Bopper in 1959.

WRITING FROM A PERSONAL PLACE

Try writing a lyric that comes from a personal place. Relate an experience you have had or an emotion you may be feeling (e.g., happy, excited, lonely, sad, hurt, missing someone).

Example
"All Alone" (Irving Berlin)

All alone, I'm so all alone
There is no one else but you
All alone by the telephone
Waiting for a ring, a ting-a-ling

I'm all alone every evening
All alone, feeling blue
Wond'ring where you are and how you are
And if you are all alone, too

USE YOUR IMAGINATION

It's fun to write songs that assume someone else's perspective. It could be a person you've never even met. Observe other people's lives and put yourself in their shoes. You can also invent characters. Give the character a name, an identity, define what they look and act like. Use your imagination to create a scenario or story.

Here are some examples of songs with made-up characters:

"Betty" (Taylor Swift) is from the perspective of a 17-year-old high-school boy named James. He loses Betty, his first girlfriend, after cheating on her.

"Pinball Wizard" (The Who) tells the story of a deaf, mute, blind boy who becomes a pinball champion and gains fame and fortune.

"Space Oddity" (David Bowie) is about a fictional character, Astronaut Major Tom, who blasts off into space but loses connection with ground control and gets lost in space. The song was released in 1969, the same year American astronauts landed on the moon. Though many people claim it was written about the lunar landing, David Bowie says he wrote it after seeing the 1968 Stanley Kubrick movie *2001: A Space Odyssey*; the song title is a play on the film's title. This is another example of a song in which the title of the song is not used in the lyric.

"Rocky Raccoon" (The Beatles) is set in the Old Wild West. Rocky is conflicted over a love triangle. Rocky's girlfriend Lil leaves him and runs off with a man named Dan. Seeking revenge, Rocky finds Dan and Lil in a hotel room and challenges Dan to a gunfight. Dan is quicker on the draw and shoots Rocky, who survives the wound and finds a Bible in his room and takes it as a sign from God.

"Wichita Lineman" (Glen Campbell) refers to a repair technician for electric or communication power lines. The writer Jimmy Webb was inspired by the apparent isolation of a solitary telephone lineman on top of a pole on an empty stretch of highway. He wrote this about a lineman in the middle of Kansas who works on telephone poles. He's devoted to his job, and he misses his girlfriend.

CHAPTER 2: SONG STRUCTURE

A song is comprised of separate parts. Most commonly, songs contain verses, choruses, and sometimes a bridge. These parts help you develop and tell a story.

SONG SECTIONS

Verse

The **verse** tells the main storyline. At least two verses are needed to develop and explore the primary idea of the song and complete the narrative, so that the listener understands what the song wishes to convey. There are usually at least two verses in a song. Each verse has a new set of lyrics.

Chorus

The lyrics of the **chorus** usually repeat the same words every time it appears. The chorus is where you want the catchiest and most memorable phrase or word; often, it is the title of the song. This is where you drive home the song's message. The title is also referred to as the **hook**, and usually is sung at the beginning or at the end of the chorus.

Bridge

The bridge usually occurs only once in the song. Musically and lyrically, it steps away from the verses and chorus. Here, a new perspective may appear that ties the song together or gives the song a clearer meaning. Not every song has or needs a bridge.

Example
"Eyes" (Tom Hambridge)

Verse
I hear voices when you sleep
I know all those secrets that you keep
On the inside
Where you hide

Chorus
My heart has eyes
It sees through lies
And late at night
It gives me sight
You can't hide
My heart has eyes

Bridge
Cry until you're dry as the desert
Cry until the well runs dry
Then you'll know what crying is
You'll know what crying is

PRE-CHORUS

Some songs include a section after the verse – and just before the chorus – that is used to connect and raise the emotional level or tension before the chorus kicks in. This is called a **pre-chorus**.

Example
"Gillian" (Tom Hambridge)

Verse
I think I died today
I think I died alone
Twenty-five miles away
About twenty-five miles from home

Pre-Chorus
And I'm fading in, and I'm fading out
Yeah, I'm fading in and I'm fading out

Chorus
There are no more words to say
I got no more notes to play
There's no more there's nothing left
I got no more words to say
No more notes to play
There's no more I ain't got nothing left
There's nothing left

SONG FORMS

The organization of the sections of a song determines its **form**. There are many different song forms; the most common are listed below. (You can always make up your own song form.) Many songwriters stick to the common forms because they are tried-and-true. They are set up to be pleasing to the ear, and the listener will be familiar with them.

When writing out song forms, we label

- Verse: A

- Chorus: B

- Bridge: C

Examples of common song forms:
ABAB
ABAC
AABAB
ABABCB
AABA
AAA

Examples of song form ABAB
"Fly Me to the Moon" (Frank Sinatra)
"Angels" (Robbie Williams)

Examples of song form ABAC
"Moon River" (Andy Williams)
"White Christmas" (Bing Crosby)

Examples of song form AABA
"What a Wonderful World" (Louis Armstrong)
"Back in the U.S.S.R." (The Beatles)
"Harlem on My Mind" (Irving Berlin)

Examples of song form AAA
"The Times They Are A-Changing" (Bob Dylan)
"Maggie May" (Rod Stewart)

Interesting fact: Genesis named their hit song "ABACAB" after the form of the song while they were writing it. Though the form changed slightly by the time they finished recording it, they kept the title nevertheless.

CHAPTER 3: WORD PLAY

ALLITERATION

Many songwriters use little word tricks in songs. **Alliteration** is the repetition of the initial consonant sound in consecutive words, such as "Peter piper picked a peck of pickled peppers." Crosby, Stills & Nash use alliteration throughout the verses in "Helplessly Hoping." Some songs use alliteration in the title and throughout the song.

Alliteration Song Title Examples
"Bad Blood" (Taylor Swift)
"Magic Man" (Heart)
"Mean Mr. Mustard" (The Beatles)
"Bell Bottom Blues" (Eric Clapton)
"White Wedding" (Billy Idol)
"Rudolph the Red-Nosed Reindeer" (Johnny Marks)

Examples of Alliteration throughout the song:
"Hard-Hearted Hannah (The Vamp of Savannah)"
To **T**ease and **t**o **T**hrill 'em
To **T**orture and kill 'em
I **s**aw her at the **s**ea **s**hore
Brother, she's a **p**olarbear's **p**ajamas

"Rock Me Right" (Tom Hambridge)
Something **s**alty and **s**weet

"This End of the Road" (Tom Hambridge)
Wagon **w**heel to the **w**hite house

METAPHORS PROVERB FUN

You can create a different meaning by taking a famous quote, idiom, or proverb and changing a word or two. The Altered Five Blues Band changed the phrase "Great minds think alike" to "Great minds drink alike." Kenny Chesney sings a song called "Time Flies (When You're Having Rum)." Obviously, the writers replaced "fun" with "rum."

Examples
"Great Minds Drink Alike" (Altered Five Blues Band)
"Time Flies (When You're Having Rum)" (Kenny Chesney)
"I've Got Friends in Low Places" (Garth Brooks)
"Eight Days a Week" (The Beatles)
"Stop! In the Name of Love" (The Supremes)

RHYME SCHEMES

Most song lyrics and poems rhyme. In songs, the rhyme usually falls on the final word of a line. The rhyme can happen at the end of two consecutive lines, or at the end of every other line, depending on the rhyme scheme you want to use.

Examples of rhyme schemes
AABB
I've waited such a long **time**
For you to be **mine**
I hope it's not too **late**
How long do I have to **wait**?

AAAA
If you're feeling **free**
you can come with **me**
Together we will **be**
Sailing on the **sea**

ABCB
Roses are red
Violets are **blue**
You love me
I love **you**

Here is an example of rhyming words in the verse, as well as rhyming the last word of the phrase:
"The Half of It Dearie Blues" (George Gershwin)
Each time you **trill** a song with **Bill** or look at **Will**
I get a **chill**, I'm *gloomy*
I won't **recall** the names of **all** the men who **fall**
It's all **appalling** *to me*

Rhyme Syllables (Examples)

One-syllable rhymes
felt
melt
welt
dealt

Two-syllable rhymes
cartwheel
unseal
surreal

Three-syllable rhymes
guarantee
disagree
bumblebee

CLOSE RHYMES

When the ending consonants of two words match, but the preceding vowel sounds do not, these are often called **close** (or **near**) **rhymes**. They also can be two words that sound the same, but do not rhyme perfectly.

Here are some close rhyme examples:
sun/gone
near/prayer
beach/clean
taste/last

PHRASING

The manner in which a singer or instrumentalist shapes or delivers the melody is called **phrasing**. You can hold a word or note longer or make it shorter. You can sing a phrase, take a breath and continue, or you can string many words together, making the phrase longer. The way you phrase or deliver your lyrics can express excitement, sadness, happiness, or aggressiveness.

CHAPTER 4: SONG TITLES

WHAT IS THE TITLE OF YOUR SONG?

The title of your song is very important. It is like a first impression. Before you play your song, someone may ask, "What's it called?" or "What's the name of the song?" Once you reveal the song title, an impression is made on the listener. You may want a memorable, catchy title in hopes people will remember it. A provocative title can achieve this.

HOW TO COME UP WITH THE TITLE

The title may be a word or line that sticks out above all the others, cluing the listener in as to the song's message. Often, the title will be obvious because it is repeated many times throughout the song. There are exceptions to every rule when writing a song, so some titles do not connect with its message. For example, you could use the city you were in when you wrote it or what the weather was like when you were inspired to create the song.

WHERE TO PLACE THE TITLE

Many times, the title of the song is sung in the chorus. The chorus is usually repeated several times throughout the song, so the title will be heard multiple times. Of course, there are exceptions to every songwriting rule.

Songs that begin the chorus with the title:
"This Love" (Maroon 5)
"Down on the Corner" (Creedence Clearwater Revival)
"Don't Let the Sun Go Down on Me" (Elton John)
"More Than a Feeling" (Boston)

Songs that have the title as the last line of the chorus:
"Before He Cheats" (Carrie Underwood)
"Stop Dragging My" Heart Around (Tom Petty)
"I'll Name the Dogs" (Blake Shelton)
"Unforgettable" (Thomas Rhett)

Songs in which the title is both the first and last lines of the chorus:
"Before You Go" (Lewis Capaldi)
"You May Be Right" (Billy Joel)
"Let It Be" (The Beatles)
"Run to You" (Bryan Adams)

In some songs, the only words in the chorus are the title of the song, sometimes repeated multiple times in the chorus.
"Hallelujah" (Leonard Cohen)
"Sunday Bloody Sunday" (U2)
"Who Can It Be Now?" (Men at Work)
"Smooth Operator" (Sade)
"Panama" (Van Halen)
"Rumor Has It" (Adele)
"I Love a Rainy Night" (Eddie Rabbit)
"You Shook Me All Night Long" (AC/DC)

These songs have the title as the opening line of the song:
"Hello It's Me" (Todd Rundgren)
"drivers license" (Olivia Rodrigo)
"I Want You to Want Me" (Cheap Trick)
"Ain't No Sunshine" (Bill Withers)
"Hello" (Adele)

"Sweet Dreams" (Eurythmics)
"Come Away with Me" (Nora Jones)
"Us And Them" (Pink Floyd)
"Lady" (Styx)
"Something" (The Beatles)
"The Long and Winding Road" (The Beatles)
"Desperado" (The Eagles)

Songs without the title anywhere in the song:
"Smells Like Teen Spirit" (Nirvana)
"Immigrant Song" (Led Zeppelin)
"Iris" (Goo Goo Dolls)
"Bohemian Rhapsody" (Queen)
"Baba O'Riley" (The Who)
"Space Oddity" (David Bowie)
"A Day in the Life" (The Beatles)
"After the Gold Rush" (Neil Young)
"Annie's Song" (John Denver)
"Everybody's Everything" (Santana)
"Goodnight Saigon" (Billy Joel)
"Hair of the Dog" (Nazareth)
"New York Mining Disaster" (Bee Gees)

In others, the title is sung at the end of every verse:
"Close to You" (Carpenters)
"New York State of Mind" (Billy Joel)
"And I Love Her" (The Beatles)
"Just The Way You Are" (Billy Joel)

"Don't Stop Believing" by Journey is an exception to most songwriting rules. The phrase "Don't Stop Believing" is the title of the song and is sung in the chorus, but the chorus doesn't occur until near the end of the song: It is over four minutes in length, but the chorus is not heard until the three-and-a-half-minute mark. This is unusual, but it worked and was and still is a huge favorite and memorable song to listeners all around the world.

The band Chicago released their first single, "Questions 67 and 68," in 1969. The title is sung only one time in the song, the last lyric you hear. Songwriter Robert Lamm said it was about a girl he knew during 1967 and 1968.

One-word song titles
"Royals" (Lorde)
"Jump" (Van Halen)
"Dreams" (Fleetwood Mac)
"Reunited" (Peaches & Herb)
"Firework" (Katy Perry)
"Radioactive" (Imagine Dragons)
"Smooth" (Santana featuring Rob Thomas)
"Kryptonite" (3 Doors Down)
"Centerfold" (J. Geils Band)
"Luka" (Suzanne Vega)

Songs with a woman's name in the title
"Billie Jean" (Michael Jackson)
"Beth" (Kiss)
"Michelle" (The Beatles)
"Rhiannon" (Fleetwood Mac)

"Rosanna" (Toto)
"Maggie Mae" (Rod Stewart)
"Mandy" (Barry Manilow)
"Sarah Smile" (Hall and Oates)
"Roxanne" (The Police)

Songs with numbers in the title
"50 Ways to Leave Your Lover" (Paul Simon)
"99 Red Balloons" (Nena)
"10,000 Hours" (Dan + Shay & Justin Bieber)
"Seven Nation Army" (White Stripes)
"Summer of '69" (Bryan Adams)
"Eight Days a Week" (The Beatles)
"Questions 67 and 68" (Chicago)
"Edge of Seventeen" (Stevie Nicks)

Songs with colors in the title
"Back in Black" (AC/DC)
"Purple Haze" (Jimi Hendrix)
"Brown-Eyed Girl" (Van Morrison)
"Yellow Submarine" (The Beatles)
"Red" (Taylor Swift)
"Yellow" (Coldplay)
"Purple Rain" (Prince)
"Brown Sugar" (Rolling Stones)

Songs with animals in the title
"Eye of the Tiger" (Survivor)
"Black Cow" (Steely Dan)
"The Lion Sleeps Tonight" (The Tokens)
"A Horse with No Name" (America)
"Crocodile Rock" (Elton John)
"Fox on the Run" (Sweet)
"Rooster" (Alice in Chains)
"Black Dog" (Led Zeppelin)

OXYMORONS

Some titles evoke wonderful play on words. **Oxymorons** combine words that have opposite meanings.

"Earth Angel" (The Penguins)
"Concrete Jungle" (Bob Marley & the Wailers)
"The Sound of Silence" (Simon & Garfunkel)
"A Hard Day's Night" (The Beatles)

CHAPTER 5: THE MUSIC SECTION

WHAT IS A CHORD? 🔊

A **chord** is the simultaneous sounding of two or more notes, usually built off a single root note. A triad is a chord made of three notes, a root note and the third and fifth above it. Seventh chords are triads that include an added seventh note. The sequence of chords used to support the melody of the song is called a chord progression.

Chord Progressions

A **chord progression** is a succession of chords built upon various notes of a musical scale. Though there are many different chord progressions, there are some proven, more common or favored ones that many songwriters gravitate to. There are also many uncommon chord progressions that may be more adventurous to the ear and stimulate more melodic ideas.

Roman Numerals for Chord Changes

Roman numerals are sometimes used to indicate chords in a song. The numerals are based on the scale or key of the song.

In the key of G major, I, V, vi, IV (1, 5, 6, 4) refer to the chords built on the first, fifth, sixth, and fourth notes of that key: G, D, Em, and C.

Typically, uppercase Roman numerals (such as I, IV, V) are used to represent major chords, while lowercase Roman numerals (such as i, iv, v) are used to represent minor chords.

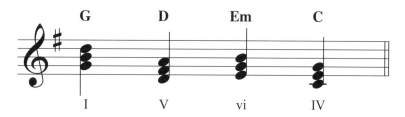

HOW MAJOR AND MINOR CHORDS DIFFER

Major chords tend to sound brighter and happier. Minor chords sound darker and sadder. A major chord contains the first, third, and fifth degree of the major scale. A minor chord contains the first, a flatted-third, and the fifth degree of the major scale of that note.

Examples of minor chord songs
"Marry You" (Bruno Mars)
"Jolene" (Dolly Parton)
"Ballin'" (Alicia Keys)
"Knockin' on Heaven's Door" (Bob Dylan)

Primary Chords

The three primary chords in a major progression are I, IV, V of the scale. (Roman numerals are used to indicate the chords). For example, in the key of C major, the primary chords are C (I), F (IV), and G (V).

The primary chords in a minor key are also based on notes 1, 4, and 5 of the minor scale. So, in the key of A minor, the notes are A, D, and E. Chord 1 is a minor chord, chord 4 is a minor chord, and chord 5 is a major chord. The primary (or i–iv –V) chords are A minor, D minor, and E major.

Common Chord Changes

One of the most-used chord progressions is C–G–A minor–F. This is used in "Let It Be" by the The Beatles.

Three-chord progressions are also quite common. They are often presented as groupings of four chords, but two of the four chords are the same.

Examples of three-chord progressions

I–IV–V–V

I–I–IV–V

I–IV–I–V

I–IV–V–IV

Many popular songs have only three chords. Here are some examples of songs with just three chords: G, C, and D.
"Sweet Home Alabama (Lynyrd Skynyrd)
"I'm Gonna Be" (500 Miles) (Proclaimers)
"Free Fallin'" (Tom Petty)
"Hang On Sloopy" (The McCoys)
"To Be with You" (Mr. Big)
"Let Her Cry" (Hootie & The Blowfish)
"Beverly Hills" (Weezer)
"La Bamba" (Richie Valens)

Here is the chord progression from "Happy Birthday," using just those three chords:

    (G)   (D)
Happy Birthday to you

    (D)   (G)
Happy Birthday to you

    (G)   (C)
Happy Birthday, dear (name)

    (D)   (G)
Happy Birthday to you.

These songs use only the chords E, A, and D:
"Born in the U.S.A." (Bruce Springsteen)
"Sweet Caroline" (Neil Diamond)
"Lean on Me" (Bill Withers)
"Walk on the Wild Side" (Lou Reed)

Many songs contain only two chords:
"Eleanor Rigby" (The Beatles): E minor and C major
"The Love Comes to Town" (U2 with B.B. King): E major and A major
"Achy Breaky Heart" (Billy Ray Cyrus): E major and A major
"A Horse with No Name" (America): E minor and D6

Blues Chord Progressions

The 12-bar blues is one of the most common chord progressions in popular music. Many traditional blues chord progressions primarily consist of the I, IV, and V chords. These can be played in many different tempos and styles: fast, slow, funky, swing, or shuffle. When these chord changes are performed at a slower tempo, they are often set in 6/8 time. This feel is commonly called "slow blues."

"Got My Mojo Working" (Muddy Waters)
C C C C   F F C C   G F C C

"I Can't Quit You Baby" (Otis Rush)
A C A A   D D A A   E D A A

"Crossroads Blues" (Robert Johnson)
A D A A   D D A A   E D A A

"Red House" (Jimi Hendrix)
B E B B   E E B B   F♯ E B F♯

"Every Day I Have the Blues" (B.B. King)
C C C C   F F C C   G F C C

"I'd Rather Go Blind" (Etta James)
A Bm Bm A   A Bm Bm A   A Bm Bm A

"C.C. RIDER" (MISSISSIPPI JOHN HURT)

Spiritual or Gospel Chord Progressions

"He's Got the Whole World in His Hands"
C C Dm Dm   C C G7 C

"Swing Low, Sweet Chariot"
F Dm Gm C7   Dm Am Gm C7   F F7 B♭ Gm   F C7 F F

"Michael Row the Boat Ashore"
C C F C   Em Dm G7 C

American Folk Chord Progressions

"House of the Rising Sun" (Anonymous)
Bm E7 F#7 Bm   Bm A7 D F#7   Bm Bm Bm G7   Bm F#7 Bm Bm

"If I Had a Hammer (The Hammer Song)" (Pete Seeger)
D D D D   D D7 A7 A7   D D Bm G D   (D G D A7 D G D A7)   D D

"Puff the Magic Dragon" (Peter, Paul and Mary)
G Bm C G   C G A7 D7   A Bm C G   D G A7 G

"This Land Is Your Land" (Woody Guthrie)
C G D7 G   C G D7 G

"Blue Moon of Kentucky" (Bill Monroe)
G G7 C7 C7   G G D7 D7   G G7 C7 C7   G D7 G G7

Traditional British Chord Progressions

"SCARBOROUGH FAIR"

"COMIN' THROUGH THE RYE"

If a bod-y meet a bod-y com-in' through the rye,
Gin a bod-y meet a bod-y com-in' frae the toon,

If a bod-y kiss a bod-y, need a bod-y cry?
Gin a bod-y greet a bod-y, need a bod-y froon? A -

Ev - 'ry las-sie has a lad-die; None, they say, ha'e I, Yet
mong the train there is a swain I dear-ly love my-sel', But

a' the lads they smile on me, When com-in' through the rye.
what's his name or what's his name, I don-na care to tell.

"ALL THROUGH THE NIGHT"

Sleep, my child, and peace at-tend Thee, all through the night;

guard-ian an-gels God will send Thee, all through the night.

Soft the drows-y hours are creep-ing, hill and vale in slum-ber sleep-ing.

God His lov-ing vig-il keep-ing, all through the night.

Uncommon Chord Progressions

"What a Wonderful World" (Louis Armstrong)
F Am B♭ Am   Gm F A7 Dm   D♭ D♭ C C7 F

"Just The Way You Are" (Billy Joel)
D Bm Gmaj7 Bm   Gmaj7 Gm D Am D7   Gmaj7 Gm D Bm E7 G G D

Well-known Chord Progressions

The I–V–vi–IV chord progression has been used in countless songs. Here are some examples:

"I'm Yours" (Jason Mraz)
"Someone Like You" (Adele)
"Complicated" (Avril Lavigne)
"Living on a Prayer" (Bon Jovi)
"Time After Time" (Cyndi Lauper)
"Whistle" (Flo Rida)

vi–V–IV–V is another popular chord progression. Here are some songs that use it:

"Sultans of Swing" (Dire Straits)
"Come Sail Away" (Styx)
"Rolling in the Deep" (Adele)
"All Along the Watchtower" (Bob Dylan)
"Girls Just Want to Have Fun" (Cyndi Lauper)

Unexpected Chords

An unexpected chord often has no common notes between the chord proceeding it or the chord following it.

In Radiohead's "Karma Police," the chorus chords are C–D–G–F♯. The F♯ stands out as an unexpected chord, creating wonderful tension.

The Beatles' "Penny Lane" includes an expected chord. It begins with a common I–VI–ii–V progression in B major. Then suddenly, a B minor chord unexpectedly appears.

B–G♯m7–C♯m7–F♯7–B–G♯m7–Bm

Pink Floyd also includes an unexpected chord in "Us and Them." The verse begins with a common I–ii progression, then it returns to the D minor chord, which seems out of place since the song begins in D major.

D–E–Dm–G

CONNECT THE MUSIC TO THE STORY

Strive to make the music fit the mood of the story you are writing about. Minor chords and/or a slower tempo can enhance a sad lyric, whereas happy-sounding chords with a sad storyline can create tension.

MODULATION 🔊

A **modulation** is a spectacular moment when the song lifts up and takes off to a higher place. Simply put, a modulation is a change of key. One of my favorite modulations occurs in "After the Love Has Gone" by Earth, Wind and Fire. This is accomplished by playing the changes the same way, but only up a step in a different key. This can make for a dramatic moment. The Beatles modulate several times in "Lucy in the Sky with Diamonds." The most common modulations are movement up a half-step, a whole-step, or a minor third. Mr. Big has a hit song called "To Be with You." It is in E major, and at the end the song modulates up a minor third to G major.

Examples
"Man in the Mirror" (Michael Jackson)
He plays the whole song in the key of G major, then near the end moves up a half-step to A-flat major.

"I Want It That Way" (The Backstreet Boys)
Modulation occurs at 2:31.

"Livin' on a Prayer" (Bon Jovi)
Modulation occurs at 3:24.

"I Want to Dance with Somebody" (Whitney Houston)
Modulation occurs at 3:37.

"I Will Always Love You" (Whitney Houston)
Modulation occurs at 3:09.

Key Changes Within the Same Song

Changing keys in a song can also be a useful tool to make a dramatic change in the song's energy. It takes the listener to a new place.

"Layla" (Derek and the Dominos) changes keys from verse to chorus. The verse is in C# minor and the chorus is in D minor.

"Unbreak My Heart" (By Toni Braxton)
The verses are in B minor and the choruses are in D minor.

CHAPTER 6: MELODY

WHAT IS A MELODY?

A melody is a group of notes you whistle, hum, or sing with your voice or play on an instrument. Melodies combine pitches and rhythms. You can change pitches from high to low or stay on one pitch for a series of words or notes. Even though melodies are made up of a series of different pitches, rhythms, and words some can be so memorable that the listener can't get it out of their head.

Examples of memorable melodies
"Sweet Caroline" (Neil Diamond)
"I Will Always Love You" (Dolly Parton; Whitney Houston)
"Don't Stop Believin'" (Journey)

STARTING WITH A MELODY

Many songwriters come up with a melody first, then choose an appropriate key and start finding chords that work well with the tune. Some melodies gravitate toward – and sound good with – particular chords. Often, you can almost hear the chord changes to a melody just by humming it out loud.

CREATING A MELODY

You don't have a song until you set your lyrics to a melody. Say or sing the lyrics. Give pitch to your words by making some words higher and some words lower. You can also break up a two-syllable word into two different pitches. You can start high, or start low.

Example
"Happy Birthday to You"
"Hap-py" is one pitch (note).
"Birth-day" is two different notes.

"I Can't Dance" (Genesis) has a two-note melody with a big jump.
"I" is a very high note and "can't dance" jumps down to the same lower note for both words.

In the Beatles' song "Yesterday," the word "yesterday" is split between with two notes.
"Yes-" is a high note.
"-ter-day" is a lower note.

Capture the Melody

Melodies can be hard to remember. Even if you are a schooled musician, they can be difficult to write down. Record the melody on your phone or another recording device.

Big Leaps or Simple Melodies

Simple melodies can be more static or straight with not much melodic movement up or down. You can use one note for a series of words.

One note or static verse melody
Examples
"Mr. Bright Side (The Killers)
"Julia (The Beatles)
"Our Song (Taylor Swift)

Big-leap melodies:
Examples
"Unchained Melody" (Righteous Brothers)
"I Will Always Love You" (Whitney Houston)
"Wuthering Heights" (Kate Bush)
"All By Myself" (Eric Carmen; Celine Dion)
"The Star-Spangled Banner"

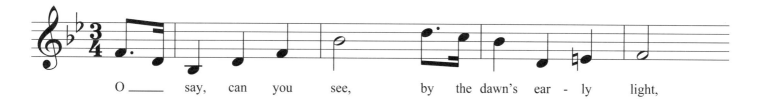

Top Line

The main melody of a song is sometimes referred to as the **top line** melody. It is essential in creating a connection with the listener. The goal is to have them walk away remembering your melody.

Rhythm of the Melody

Each syllable of your melody has a note value. Long, short, fast. You can sing some lyrics fast or hold a note for a long time, increasing the duration of the word or syllable. You can highlight or stress a word to put more emphasis on that word.

Example
The hymn "Amazing Grace" includes five notes for the word "a-maz-ing": a quarter note, a half note, and a three-note triplet.

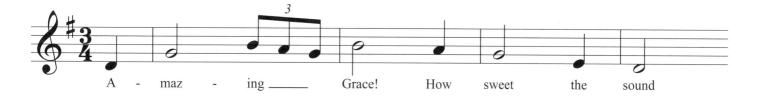

Example
In the Christmas carol "Silent Night," "Si-lent" has three different rhythmic values in the melody.

Example

Dynamics of Your Melody

Dynamics in music is moving from loud to soft or changing tempos. Queen's "Bohemian Rhapsody" is a perfect example of ways to effectively pull this off in a song. There are quiet sections, hard rock sections, and a classical section. The song also shifts keys and tempos.

Example

Another example of using dynamics in your melody by moving from soft to loud is "The House of the Rising Sun" by the Animals. The singer Eric Burdon sings the first verse soft and calm as he begins the sad story. Throughout the song he sings louder and more aggressive until on the last verse of the song (which is the first verse repeated) he screams the melody up a full octave to create an amazing emotional dynamic.

Connect the Chords to the Melody

Chords may be chosen to fit a melody you've created, or you can choose a common chord progression and try to come up with a melody to fit over the sound of the chords.

Play a Chord and Hear a Melody

Play a chord and start singing your melody. Then move to another chord. Some melodies work over many different chords. Use the chords that match your melody and are pleasing to your ear.

Exercise
Play a C chord for four bars then play an F chord for two bars then play a G chord for two bars. Try singing your melody over these chords.

CHAPTER 7: RHYTHM

COMPONENTS OF RHYTHM

Rhythm is the pattern and placement of sounds within the song. It includes how long you hold a word or a note, and the intensity with which you sing or play the note. Rhythm consists of many elements including beats, tempos, accents, phrasing and even silence.

Measures

When writing music, a **measure** (sometimes called a bar) is a specific amount of time that corresponds to a specific number of notes or beats.

Time Signatures 🔊

Time signatures tell you how many beats or pulses are in each measure or bar of music.

4/4 is the most common time signature. This lets you know that there are four beats to each measure.

3/4 time signature indicates there are three beats per measure.

Often, the strumming rhythm in a 3/4 time signature is one chord per measure. The chords usually change on Beat 1 of the measure.

Examples of 4/4 time
"Beat It" (Michael Jackson)
"Smells Like Teen Spirit" (Nirvana)
"Satisfaction" (Rolling Stones)
"I Will Survive" (Gloria Gaynor)
"Paradise City" (Guns N' Roses)

Examples of 3/4 time
"Come Away with Me" (Nora Jones)
"Are You Lonesome Tonight" (Elvis Presley)
"I'll Be" (Edward McCain)
"Breakaway" (Kelly Clarkson)

Beat

In music, the word **beat** has many meanings. For our songwriting purposes, the beat is the pulse, the feel, or groove of the song. There are many different kinds of beats: a rock beat, a funky beat, a hip-hop beat, or a reggae beat. You can even create or make up your own beat.

Examples of funky beat songs
"Uptown Funk" (Mark Ronson featuring Bruno Mars)
"Don't Stop Till U Get Enough" (Michael Jackson)
"Brick House" (The Commodores)

Examples of hip-hop beats
"Lose Yourself" (Eminem)
"Fight the Power" (Public Enemy)

Example of rock beats
"We Will Rock You" (Queen)
"Back in Black" (AC/DC)
"Eye of the Tiger" (Survivor)

Find a Tempo

The **tempo** is the speed of the song. There are fast songs, medium-tempo songs, and slow songs. The songwriter decides what tempo feels right for the song. Slow songs are referred to as **ballads**. Fast songs are called **up-tempo**. Songs that contain lots of words may be hard to sing if the tempo is too fast.

Ballad examples
"Come Away with Me" (Norah Jones)
"(Somewhere) Over the Rainbow" (from *The Wizard of Oz*)

Example of up-tempo songs
"Single Ladies" (Put a Ring on it) (Beyonce)
"Rock and Roll" (Led Zeppelin)
"Hard to Explain" (The Strokes)
"Highway Star" (Deep Purple)

Metronome

The speed of the music can be measured in beats per minute by a device called a **metronome**. When set at a specific tempo, this handy tool produces a clicking sound at an exact interval or BPM (beats per minute) that allows you to play your song at the correct tempo from beginning to end. A lot of modern music is recorded to a metronome. In recording sessions, the metronome is sometimes referred to as a "click track." All the musicians and singers play along with the click to stay in perfect time.

CHAPTER 8: GETTING DEEPER

IMAGERY

Imagery means using descriptive or figurative language to call to mind a person, place, or thing. When you look at a painting, you see everything. When you're listening to a song, you can't see the picture unless you use imagery to help paint it. The listener should be able to see what you are describing in your song lyric. If you are talking about a "road," describe it. Is it a winding road? A rough road? A long road? An open road? A gravel road? A dirt road? A back road? A hard road? Try to create a mental picture of the events as vividly as possible. A song can come to life with the right words and imagery.

Songs that use imagery
"Firework" (Katy Perry)
"Slow Dancing in a Burning Room" (John Mayer)
"Goodnight Saigon" (Billy Joel)

Metaphors

Metaphors compare two unlike elements without using "like" or "as." They can also add color to liven up the lyrics. Here are some examples:

"The Dance" (Garth Brooks)
The lyric compares a one-song dance to an entire life.

"Hotel California" (The Eagles)
The short-lived glitz and glamour of being famous is compared to staying one night in a Hollywood hotel.

"Smoke" (A Thousand Horses)
This song compares a girl to smoking a cigarette. She's the smoke. He can't put her down, he can't quit her, he's addicted to her. She is a habit he can't let go of.

"Waterfalls" (TLC)
Waterfalls is a metaphor warning us not to chase after beautiful things like waterfalls, because they can end up hurting you.

"Every Rose Has Its Thorn" (Poison) uses the rose as a metaphor for a woman. She can be beautiful to look at, but you may get hurt holding her too tight.

In "The Last Rose of Summer" by Thomas Moore, a single surviving flower serves as a metaphor for a person who outlives all their family and friends, and the sadness of being alone when everyone they knew and loved is gone.

'Tis the last rose of summer,
Left blooming alone;
All her lovely companions
Are faded and gone;
No flower of her kindred,
No rosebud is nigh,
To reflect back her blushes
Or give sigh for sigh!

So soon may I follow,
When friendships decay,
And from love's shining circle
The gems drop away!
When true hearts lie withered,
And fond ones are flown,
Oh! Who would inhabit
This bleak world alone?

Personification

Personification means giving human characteristics to something non-human; for example, writing that a lion "laughed" or a mountain "cried."

In the famous Irish folksong "Danny Boy," the author begins the story with "O Danny Boy, the pipes, the pipes are calling." The Welsh song "All Through the Night" includes the personification "While the moon her watch is keeping."

Examples of personification used in songs
"Danny Boy"
The pipes are calling

"All Through the Night"
The moon her watch is keeping

"While My Guitar Gently Weeps" (The Beatles)

Similes

A **simile** is a figure of speech that draws comparison to two unlike items with the help of the words "like" or "as." In the Simon & Garfunkel song "Bridge Over Troubled Water," the simile shows how a friend will support another friend, no matter what. This compares the emotional support of one friend to another in difficult times, to a physical bridge over rough water below.

Examples of songs with similes
"You're as Cold as Ice" (Foreigner)
"Like a Rolling Stone" (Bob Dylan)
"Like a Rock" (Bob Seger)
"Bridge Over Troubled Water" (Simon & Garfunkel)

Songs with Lists

Another lyric idea is to create a list of places, people or things with a common theme. Geoff Mack wrote a great list song, "I've Been Everywhere." In it, he names all the places he has visited, including Chicago, Oklahoma, Fargo, Tampa, and on and on. In the song "We Didn't Start the Fire," Billy Joel chronicles over 50 years of world events – from sports to entertainment to politics – in chronological order in under four-and-a-half minutes.

Examples of list songs
"It's the End of the World as We Know It" (R.E.M.)
"We Didn't Start the Fire" (Billy Joel)
"I've Been Everywhere" (Hank Snow)
"50 Ways to Leave Your Lover" (Paul Simon)

CHAPTER 9: PUTTING IT ALL TOGETHER

NO RULES

Songwriting is like anything: the more you work the muscle, the stronger or easier it gets. The only rule in songwriting is that there are no rules. If it sounds good to your ear and you like the song, it's possible that other listeners will like it as well.

People Forget

Many great ideas are lost because they were not documented. You never know when inspiration might hit you, so when you get an idea for a song, sing the melody or speak the words into the recorder on your phone. It's worth writing the idea down or recording it right away, even if you don't have time to write or complete the idea. If you record or document it, when you sit down later to write or co-write a song, you can refer to these song ideas.

Start

To get started, set aside some time each day to sit with your thoughts and ideas, and start the process of trying to create a song. Dive in and start working. Don't think about writing a song, just start writing the song.

Finish

A lot of songwriters start a song and leave it to be completed later, but they never finish it. They end up with half-written or unfinished songs. A half-written song is not a song. My advice is to complete the song, even if it's not as perfect as you want it to be. You can always change a line or two later, but at least you have a completed thought. Have fun and go for it.

RANDOM FINAL THOUGHTS

"Never My Love" (The Association)

Just reading the title, we might think that someone is making a vow never to fall in love or give his love away. The songwriters cleverly use the title to confirm to their partner that if there is any doubt that he would leave the relationship, the answer is no, or "Never My Love."

Consider using minor chords in a song to create a more serious, deeper, or sadder sound. Alternatively, major sounding chords can make your song sound happier or uplifting.

You don't have to be sad to write a sad song, and you don't have to be happy to write a happy song.

Record your song on your phone and listen back to it. Does the story or point make sense? Are the words precise enough that you would understand what the song is trying to say, even if someone else had written it?

Lyric Content

Some songs are feel-good songs. They make you smile. The subject matter in the lyrics is positive or uplifting.

Examples of feel-good songs
"Uptown Funk" (Mark Ronson)
"Shake It Off" (Taylor Swift)
"Shape of You" (Ed Sheeran)

Examples of sad songs
"I Cry" (Usher)
"Someone Like You" (Adele)
"I'm Not the Only One" (Sam Smith)

Put the Listener in the Song

Write about things people can relate to. Most everybody falls in love, tries to make a living, drives a car, has dreams. Writing about universal themes puts the listener in the song.

If it sounds good, it is good.

It's great when a songwriter remembers, forgets, or breaks all the rules and writes something that becomes a huge hit, and nobody is sure why. Many songs become hits by songwriters – like yourself – who are not very sure how to even write a song. "Take Me There," a song by Rascal Flatts, comes to mind. In the verses, they give away the hook or title and use it all through the verse. It still feels perfect when it is used as the first and last line of the chorus, because nobody cares about the rules if it sounds good. The feeling of the song shines though. The songwriter honestly and purely wants to know everything about this girl he just met, and may be falling in love with.

I love writing songs and I'm always trying to find new ways to get better at it. I hope this book helps get your songwriting juices flowing, and inspires you to put pen to paper or voice memo in phone and write songs. Who knows? Maybe you will get an idea from reading this book and write a song that changes the world. "Imagine" that!

I'm all ears. TH